The 2 Minute MIRACLE

The 2 Minute MIRACLE

Releasing God's Power,
Protection and Prosperity
with Spoken Blessings

REVISED EDITION

M. Lynn Reddick, Ph.D.

THE 2 MINUTE MIRACLE

Published by:
Portal Publishing Company
304 Grady Street
P.O. Box 399
Portal, Georgia 30450
912-865-9811
email: info@openchurch.com

We want to hear from you. Please send your comments and/or
experiences to us in care of the address above. Thank you.

Order more copies of this book at www.openchurch.com

International Standard Book Number: 0-9743297-0-3

To my wife, Linda,
God's blessing to this generation
and
my mother, Annie Laura Reddick,
matriarch of the Reddick family

PREFACE

Dear Reader,

You are about to make a discovery that will change your life and the lives of those around you. The road map you hold in your hand will lead you to a hidden treasure so powerful that you'll wonder how you've lived without it.

You are about to learn how to release God's power by speaking blessings into someone's life—even in the context of hurt feelings. And as your words begin to change lives rather miraculously, your life will change too!

You'll begin to see:

- deeper meaning in your life
- hidden potential released
- major roadblocks removed
- seemingly impossible situations turned around.

I've seen blessings restore the friendship of two single women, save the marriage of a wife ready to call it quits, and change the life of a teenager who was thinking about jumping off a bridge.

The following pages will lead you past persistent obstacles, familiar detours, and annoying delays. You will finally discover the key to unlocking the storehouse of blessings for you and others.

If you're ready, let's begin The 2 Minute Miracle.

M. Lynn Reddick, Ph.D.

PREFACE TO THE REVISED EDITION

In this edition of *The 2 Minute Miracle*, selected quotes from the text have been pulled out and emphasized on the page to highlight some of the key points made in this book.

Also, we have taken the twelve times a blessing is needed most from chapter four and supplemented each one with a foundational concept that helps clarify and underscore the importance of blessings at these significant times in our lives.

May the Lord bless and enrich your life as you in turn bless and enrich the lives of those around you.

M. Lynn Reddick, Ph.D.

ACKNOWLEDGMENTS

On a mountaintop in Colorado, the teachings of Dr. Karl D. Coke opened my eyes to the life-changing power of blessing. This revelation set my wife, Linda, and me on a journey—learning, teaching, and demonstrating how people are radically changed, often in moments, when blessings are spoken into their lives.

Jim Rutz of Colorado Springs not only financed these seminars across North America but later unselfishly placed me in the presidency of Open Church Ministries. My gratitude to him is without measure.

A group of theologians has significantly enriched my life and stirred many thoughts expressed in this book. Drs. Karl Coke, Cifford Denton, John Garr, John Looper, and Doug Wheeler have given insightful wisdom about blessing on the "ancient paths" of our biblical heritage.

As you read about blessing you will probably sense the strong family heritage to which I am deeply indebted—from grandparents who frequently blessed me on their back porch—to our grandchildren, Kayla, Ethan, and Sarah, who are learning to bless at an early age.

The Psalmist declared, "Sons are a heritage from the Lord" (127:3). Without the able help of our son Greg, this book would still be a faint dream. His literary skills and provocative questions and comments repeatedly drove me back to my writing desk.

The fingerprints and inspired breath of my companion of nearly forty years are all over this work. I bless Linda as God's gift to this generation.

CONTENTS

Never pay back one wrong with another,
or an angry word with another one;
instead, pay back with a blessing.
This is what you are called to do,
so that you inherit a blessing yourself.
1 PETER 3:9, *The Jerusalem Bible*

ONE

WHY FORGIVING
ISN'T ENOUGH

WHEN I FIRST MET CHUCK, he was climbing the ladder of success rapidly. And why not? His good looks and great personality endeared him to others, and he excelled as a gifted singer, baseball player, and college student.

He was close to his family, especially his larger-than-life grandfather, who was the center of his life from early childhood. This man didn't mince words, however, especially in voicing his expectations of his grandson.

Over the period of a few weeks in his freshman year, several unusual events converged on Chuck at one time. He scored badly on an exam, quit a part-time job, and decided against a professional baseball career. This news reached his grandfather the same weekend Chuck dropped by for a visit.

A barrage of harsh criticism met Chuck at the door, more intense than anything before. Repeatedly, his grandfather demeaned him, told him he was no good, and that he would never amount to anything. These words took root in Chuck's

mind and emotions. After his grandfather died unexpectedly
a few weeks later, they began to grow.

> Our highly developed
> nervous system makes us
> especially vulnerable to
> hurtful words and actions.

Over time these grand-
parental word-curses would
alter Chuck's identity (who he
was) and destiny (where he'd
go). Laughter was the first to
leave, followed by his interest
in music, then his involvement
with the local church. After
dropping out of college, he
began to vacillate from one job to another, and years later,
from one wife to another. Buried hurts produced a life cursed
by a grandfather whom Chuck couldn't forgive.

BURIED HURTS FROM UNFORGIVENESS

Our highly developed central nervous system makes us
especially vulnerable to hurtful words and actions. Given this
propensity for emotional injury—or soul wounds—combined with our innate fallen nature, it's not surprising that
we tend to *nurse* a hurt by mental brooding, to *rehearse* the
hurt with other people, or *curse* the hurt through blame,
rather than *reverse* the hurt by forgiving.

An emotional quagmire soon develops:

> An **insult** leads to **injury**, which naturally stirs
> **anger** (conscious or unconscious), resulting in a
> **refusal to forgive**, which breeds **resentment** or
> hate, which produces a **curse** (physical, emotional,
> and spiritual harm) on the person's life.

The mind is unable to feel pain, so emotional hurts pass on to the body for either burial *or* resolution. Don't think, however, that burial means gone for good. Buried hurts become planted in the soil of the subconscious and often sprout in bodily symptoms. In other words, the body reveals what the mind conceals.

> The body reveals what the mind conceals.

A good analogy of this is a childhood experience I had on our farm in Georgia. I attempted a shortcut in my pea-planting chores one afternoon by burying a whole bucket of peas at the end of a row. I came home from school a few days later to discover a note from Dad telling me to meet him in the pea patch. I found him there riding the one-row tractor. I walked closer and saw the peas were sprouting nice and green and tall. Then, like an explosion, it caught my eye—down at the end of the row: the biggest outcropping of a pea-bush anybody ever saw. It was a terrible sight for my eight-year-old eyes. Needless to say, what I thought was buried had come back to haunt me in a big way.

When someone is emotionally hurt and withholds forgiveness, resentment begins to germinate deep within like buried seeds. Hate soon emerges in one form or another.

The Bible doesn't distinguish between resentment and hate because of the fine line separating them. Hate is such an intensive, destructive emotion that the Bible even equates it with murder.

> Anyone who hates his brother is a murderer, and
> you know that no murderer has eternal life in him.
> — 1 JOHN 3:15

Resentment becomes a buried seed that produces the fruit of bitterness, depression, and physical illness, often disguising itself in the clothes of justification: "I have the right to feel this way." However, resentment becomes a curse in four areas:

- Physically, it can contribute to illnesses such as stomach ulcers, arthritis, headaches, skin rashes, and cancers.
- Emotionally, it will poison the mind and defile the mouth.
- Socially, it can destroy our closest friendships, including those with spouse and children.
- Spiritually, it will destroy our relationship with God.

The misery and torment caused by hate are characteristic of evil in the world, and especially Satan, who seeks to inflict misery on everything God creates. Hate is so destructive that God created hell to isolate Satan and hate in the future.

> Then he will say to those on his left, "Depart from me, you who are cursed, into the eternal fire prepared for the devil and his angels."
> — MATTHEW 25:41

Everyone who allows hate to take root and rule their lives is destined for this abyss of unimaginable torment.

All of us have at one time or another received an insult from another and felt the stirrings of anger—and it was at precisely that moment that we made a decision, conscious or unconscious, within ourselves. We could either harbor that insult or redirect the energy in a positive way.

If we refuse to forgive, resentment can grow into hate and produce curses, which, whether spoken once or often, help shape a person's identity and destiny, as in the case of Chuck.

DECISIVE MOMENTS

Ideally, no one can insult us unless we allow those words to affect us. However, most people don't live in this realm of reality. So, what happens when an insult causes emotional injury and stirs anger? A soul wound brings us to moments of decision: Do we forgive or do we withhold forgiveness? Either decision determines our long-term physical, emotional, and spiritual health.

If the negative effects of unforgiveness are so consequential, why doesn't everyone choose to forgive? Human nature and alienation from God are major barriers. After evil entered the human experience, responding with eye-for-eye and tooth-for-tooth is easier than forgiving.

People reconnected to God through Jesus the Messiah have an advantage in decisive moments because the indwelling Holy Spirit helps "in our weakness" (Romans 8:26). However, working through negative feelings is another matter, as I discovered a few years ago when the Lord nudged my wife and me to go to Atlanta and start a new church.

> Whether or not we choose to forgive someone determines our long-term physical, emotional, and spiritual health.

The Spirit of God directed us to a financially depressed area where we connected with three families. One of the couples helped us start the new church. Over the next two years, they became our best friends.

One Saturday we had what I thought was a minor disagreement about the direction the church should take. The following day, as the church family gathered for singing and open sharing, my best friend chose to embarrass me before the congregation. The verbal hand grenade was a public breech of friendship that shook the congregation.

In the midst of the ensuing crisis, the Lord spoke to my inner being.

Forget the hurt. Forgive the man.
But Lord, He didn't tell the whole story.
Forget the hurt. Forgive the man.
But Lord . . .

Forgiving during times of increase was easier than times of decrease as the congregation scattered like a covey of quail. What a struggle it was to choose forgiveness over anger in the face of what felt like utter betrayal!

I finally decided to drive by my ex-friend's house and speak forgiveness—from the road. Honestly, at the time, I didn't expect this distant pardon to mend our relationship, but I did know that I was sitting on a lot of pent up frustrations, or, more to the point, anger, that could either be held onto or released; and knowing what I knew about the consequences of emotional baggage, I needed to forgive this man. To my surprise, he actually phoned a year later to express regret for the manner in which he had conducted himself before the congregation. A result of my drive-by blessings? Perhaps.

The conversation was brief. I accepted his apology. But the deep emotional wound produced a scar that still itched at times. After three years, thinking I had completely worked through any resentment, I saw a man in a parking lot that closely resembled my ex-friend. When a cold chill swept over me, I knew there was more buried hurt within. No wonder Jesus came to heal our broken hearts!

Yes, Lord. I understand. Keep forgiving.

Four years after the verbal ambush, I dropped by a building supply company and headed down an aisle near the back of the warehouse. The only two shoppers at the far end did not notice me approaching at first, but as I got within thirty feet, their heads raised. For the first time in four years, our eyes met. The hair on the back of my neck didn't bristle. Nothing coiled up inside my chest. As I got closer, an almost supernatural peace seemed to cover me like a mantle.

Brushing aside his outstretched hand, I gave him our customary bear hug. Then, I warmly greeted his wife, just like old times. This warehouse reunion didn't quite restore our friendship, but for me, it demonstrated God's power to finally heal my soul wounds.

HEALING SOUL WOUNDS

It began in Jerusalem as the Jews gathered for an eight-day celebration of Passover, Unleavened Bread, and Firstfruits. These festive holidays brought a well-known itinerant prophet-healer and his disciples to the city. Gathering in an upstairs room, this widely acclaimed Messiah (Anointed One—Our Savior) ate the ancient Passover meal with twelve of his followers. They remembered the mighty acts of God in Egypt when death swept over that nation, killing the first-born of every man and animal, but passing over Hebrew (later known as Jewish) families.

All went well at the supper table until Jesus began speaking strange words about betrayal, blood, suffering, and death. The following three-day Jerusalem nightmare darkened all Messianic hopes when his disciples saw their carpenter hanging lifeless between two criminals.

Hopelessness spread like a plague across Jerusalem. Despondency and fear drove the remaining eleven men into a locked dining room, out of harm's way from the Jewish authorities. Imagine the shock when a ghost-like figure, passing through a wall, stood in front of them and said, "Shalom!" By that time this motley group needed peace.

With amazement these disciples finally realized that this really was Jesus the Messiah, *alive*. Disbelief slowly lifted as sorrow became joy and despair gave way to hope. Soon, fearful cowards would become courageous power teams throughout the known world.

But not without a price.

It wasn't long before severe persecution broke out. What should a person do in the face of such hostilities? Pay back by trying to get even?

> We must pay back a hurtful deed or angry words with blessings.

Peter wrote encouraging words to those who were walking through difficulty, disappointment, pain, and suffering. He charts a different course for these early believers—and us—by suggesting that we must pay back a wrong deed or angry words with blessings.

> Never pay back one wrong with another, or an angry word with another one; instead, pay back with a blessing. This is what you are called to do, so that you inherit a blessing yourself.
> — 1 PETER 3:9, *The Jerusalem Bible*

Before we can sincerely bless someone, we must forgive them of any emotional wounds they might have inflicted.

This principle can be traced back three thousand years to the Proverbs of a king named Solomon. "If a man pays back evil for good, evil will never leave his house" (17:13). "Do not say, 'I'll pay back for this wrong!' Wait for the LORD, and he will deliver you" (20:22).

If we forgive,
we will be forgiven.

These axioms of revenge, planted in the soil of human history, sprouted a thousand years later and developed into major principles of forgiveness by Jesus. He taught that if we hold anything against anyone, we must forgive them so we will be forgiven by God.

> And when you stand praying, if you hold anything against anyone, forgive him, so that your Father in heaven may forgive you your sins.
> — MARK 11:25-26

We must forgive so we will be forgiven.

If we choose to forgive—not based on how we feel about the person or what was said, but on our decision to take no offense—an emotional timeline of forgiveness unfolds:

> An **insult** leads to **injury**, which naturally stirs **anger** (conscious or unconscious) and brings us to a *decision*. **Forgiveness** extends **acceptance and love** that result in **blessings**.

Although we can initiate forgiveness with a decision, God has to work within us to heal our soul wounds and stir acceptance and love for the offender. What we initiate with a decision, He cultivates by His Spirit to bring us to the point of heartfelt forgiveness. Forgiving and blessing open the door to *our* blessings.

Perhaps this is why these empowered believers "turned the world upside down" (Acts 17:6, *King James Version*), at least for the first two hundred years. They learned the love-response of forgiving and speaking blessings instead of curses. Forgiving and blessing others released God's hand of blessings in their lives.

> Forgiving and blessing others releases God's hand of blessing.

Quite a life-principle, as Mike discovered one day. It started out like any other Sunday as our church family gathered to worship. That particular morning I spoke on the power of forgiveness, urging everyone to replace resentment with spoken blessings.

Mike was among the first to request help. An older couple took him aside to discuss his needs. I walked over just in time to hear Mike tell how worthless he felt. Not only did his mother give him away at birth, she never contacted him even one time.

For thirty-four years, he lived without any knowledge of his mother, where she was or even if she was alive. Rejection, inferiority, guilt, and resentment plagued his life. A loving wife and two children didn't ease the pain of worthlessness very much.

The counseling couple discussed the need to speak forgiveness to his absent mother. They placed an empty chair in front of Mike.

"Tell your mother how you feel," they said.

Soon, Mike began speaking out from his heart. "Mom," he said. "I forgive you for giving me away. But I'm so lonely. If I could just hear your voice, feel your touch, know that you love me. I bless you as my mother and ask God to release you from guilt and any condemnation."

The next morning, someone knocked at my office door. There stood Mike.

"I forgave and blessed my mother yesterday," he said, "not only at the end of our church meeting, but all afternoon, and you will never believe what happened during supper last night."

"What happened?" I asked.

"The phone rang. It was my mother."

He paused for a moment, overcome with emotion, then he continued: "She asked me to forgive her."

This story, unimaginable but true, demonstrates the power of forgiving and blessing, even at a distance.

NUTS, BOLTS, AND WASHERS

Forget the $100. Forgive and bless the man.
But Lord, do you know what he did to me?
Forget the $100. Forgive and bless the man.
But, Lord . . .

After high school graduation, I spent the summer in my hometown of Portal working at the Recreation Department, a job paying an astonishing $100 per week. Not much today, but for an eighteen-year-old in 1961 it was quite a lot.

Problem was, Larry, who wrote my weekly checks, overlooked paying me the last $100. I brooded over this incident so much that my hurt hardened into resentment. To further compound the problem, I had to pass his house to get almost anywhere from mine. Even going to college didn't help much. Home on weekends, I'd drive by Larry's house only to experience an onslaught of negative thoughts and feelings.

I sensed the Lord saying to me, *Forget the $100. Forgive*

and bless him. So, when feelings of resentment rose up, I'd remind myself that I had decided to forgive and bless Larry. I would quietly speak as if he was standing near, "I forgive you and bless you with the Spirit of God. May He prosper you and draw you to Himself."

Eventually, I *forgot* the $100.

When I became president of a Christian organization in Colorado, office furnishings were moved from Colorado Springs and stored near my home in Georgia until a new office location was determined.

A few months later, sitting in my truck in the middle of my hometown of about one thousand residents, I looked at a vacant building directly in front of me. The Familiar Voice inside me said, *That is the building.*

A phone call arranged the meeting. I explained the vision and ministry my wife and I were called to do.

Questions followed, including one of mine. "Why hasn't the building been rented for years?"

I was told that there were about seventy-five tons of nuts, bolts, and washers in that place. And the owners didn't know what to do with them.

> The God of provision is constantly looking for people He can bless and use to bless others.

"Why don't you put them in small bags and sell them to local farmers at a cut-rate," I suggested.

Two weeks passed. Then I heard from the owners:

"Lynn, we've reached a decision. We want to give your organization the building."

In four weeks, all of the nuts, bolts, and washers had been sold. A miracle in itself.

Driving back from the attorney's office with the property

deed in hand, I sensed the Lord say rather suddenly, *Son, remember the $100.*

These words were so shockingly real that I pulled off onto the shoulder of the highway. Looking over on my right, I realized that I was sitting in front of a familiar house—the house of Larry Smith who, forty years earlier, never paid me that last $100.

Larry and Joann Smith had just given us the $100,000 building in the middle of town—one that would become the headquarters of an international ministry and Bible college.

The Lord's presence filled the truck cab as tears welled up in my eyes. I heard Him say, *Because you forgave and learned to bless Larry, today I have taken that $100 and turned it into $100,000.*

This incident is about more than nuts, bolts, and washers. It's about struggling to forgive and learning to speak blessings in the place of brooding resentment. It's about the God of provision who is constantly looking for people He can bless and use to bless other people.

In the next chapter you will discover what blessing is, as well as the source. You'll be awed by the powerful, mysterious, and supernatural impact spoken blessings have, often in a matter of minutes.

took the remainder of the class period to finish their assignment. As the students left the room, each one handed me their paper. Mark said, "Thank you for teaching me, Sister. Have a good weekend."

That Saturday, I wrote down the name of each student on a separate sheet of paper, and I listed what everyone else had said about that individual. On Monday I gave each student his or her list. Before long, the entire class was smiling.

"Really?" I heard whispered.

"I never knew that meant anything to anyone!"

"I didn't know others liked me so much."

No one ever mentioned those papers in class again. I never knew if they discussed them after class or with their parents, but it didn't matter. The exercise had accomplished its purpose. The students were happy with themselves and one another again.

That group of students moved on. Several years later, after I returned from vacation, my parents met me at the airport. As we were driving home, Mother asked me the usual questions about the trip, the weather, my experiences in general. There was a lull in the conversation. Mother gave Dad a sideways glance and simply said, "Dad?" My father cleared his throat as he usually did before saying something important.

"The Eklunds called last night," he began.

"Really?" I said. "I haven't heard from them in years. I wonder how Mark is."

Dad responded quietly. "Mark was killed in Vietnam," he said. "The funeral is tomorrow, and his parents would like it if you could attend."

To this day I can still point to the exact spot on I-494 where Dad told me about Mark.

I had never seen a serviceman in a military coffin before. Mark looked so handsome, so mature. All I could think at that moment was, *Mark, I would give all the masking tape in the world if only you would talk to me.*

The church was packed with Mark's friends. Chuck's sister sang "The Battle Hymn of the Republic." Why did it have to rain on the day of the funeral? It was difficult enough at the graveside. The priest said the usual prayers, and the bugler played taps. One by one those who loved Mark took a last walk by the coffin and sprinkled it with holy water.

I was the last one to bless the coffin. As I stood there, one of the soldiers who acted as pallbearer came up to me. "Were you Mark's math teacher?" he asked. I nodded as I continued to stare at the coffin.

"Mark talked about you a lot," he said.

After the funeral, most of Mark's former classmates headed to Chuck's farmhouse for lunch. Mark's mother and father were there, obviously waiting for me. "We want to show you something," his father said, taking a wallet out of his pocket. "They found this on Mark when he was killed. We thought you might recognize it."

Opening the billfold, he carefully removed two worn pieces of notebook paper that had obviously been taped, folded and refolded many times. I knew without looking that the papers were the ones on which I had listed all the good things each of Mark's classmates had said about him.

"Thank you so much for doing that," Mark's mother said. "As you can see, Mark treasured it."

Mark's classmates started to gather around us. Charlie smiled rather sheepishly and said, "I still have my list. It's in the top drawer of my desk at home."

Chuck's wife said, "Chuck asked me to put his in our wedding album."

Then Vicki, another classmate, reached into her pocketbook, took out her wallet and showed her worn and frazzled list to the group. "I carry this with me at all times," Vicki said without batting an eyelash. "I think we all saved our lists."

That's when I finally sat down and cried. I cried for Mark and for all his friends who would never see him again.

If folded pieces of paper with affirmations can have such impact, imagine the powerful effect words have, not written once but spoken repeatedly!

The God of the universe is the source of blessings and calls us to a lifestyle of giving and receiving blessings from His storehouse.

WHAT BLESSING IS ALL ABOUT

Bless derives its meaning from Old and New Testament words *barak* and *eulogeo* respectively. While both have the meaning "to pronounce blessed," *barak* means to convey a gift with a powerful utterance as God did over His creation (Genesis 1:22, 28). *Eulogeo,* from which we get the word "eulogy," means to speak well of (*eu,* "well," *logos,* "a word"), cause to benefit from material things (Hebrews 6:7; 2 Corinthians 9:5), and to make happy and prosperous (Galatians 3:9; Ephesians 1:3).

The Amplified New Testament expands the meaning of blessing to include "welfare, happiness, and protection" (1

Peter 3:9). **Speaking blessings can release God's power, goodness, favor, and protection.** Each of Paul's New Testament letters closes with a blessing pronounced upon both hearers and readers.

God first spoke blessings over His creation by releasing His power and purpose in both animals and people: "Be fruitful and increase in number" (Genesis 1:22, 28). This set the tone of God's favor toward creation as a loving Father who desired to pour out His love and favor upon us. Later, He sent His one-of-a-kind Son to show everyone His goodness and mercy. Thus, from the beginning of creation He revealed His desire to bless.

Releasing God as the Source

Sneeze in Israel and they say, "To your health." Germans say, "Good health." Where English is spoken it is, "God Bless you." All these sneeze-responses mean the same: "I see by your sneeze that you may be getting sick. I bless you with good health."

> When we bless, something living and active is released in the invisible world around us that brings positive benefits.

While this biblical concept acknowledges God as the source of blessings, we transmit His power, goodness, favor, and protection by speaking blessings into other people's lives. Our authority to bless can be seen in Jesus' instruction to "let your peace rest upon the home" (Matthew 10:13).

One of the best-known examples of a father's blessing is found in Genesis 27 where Isaac's blessing for his son Jacob consists of the power of life, fertility, and prosperity.

Later, the New Testament included the idea of well-being and happiness.

When we bless, something living and active is released in the invisible world around us that brings positive benefits to someone. Through blessings, God can touch and stir something within the person that He might have spoken or stirred previously.

My wife and I were teaching in a three-day seminar a few years ago when she received a strong impression that a middle-aged businessman present was running from God's call on his life. Later in the meeting she blessed him as a man of God with a divine call on his life.

"Wasn't there a time when you felt God wanted you to be a pastor?" she asked.

"Absolutely not! God has never given me such an impression," he said, and returned to his seat.

I was a bit apprehensive the second night when the same man returned to the meeting. As we started, he lifted his hand and asked to address the group.

"When Linda blessed me as a man called by God, I thought that was absurd. But last night I dreamed I was sitting in a clump of trees behind my house reading my Bible. I felt like the Lord spoke to my heart and called me to be a pastor. When I woke up, I remembered that actually happened when I was eight years old. But I didn't want anything to do with church or God, so I forgot the experience. I guess I buried it in my subconscious. Last night, Linda's blessing stirred something deep within me."

So, blessing can release God's hand in a person's life, especially when we bless in line with God's wishes and in the context of family and community.

Roots in the Past

Our ancient ancestors Adam and Eve lost their relationship or walk with God and faced a hopeless future of alienation. A divine-initiated covenant of love with a man named

---

Blessings aren't mere gift certificates.

Abraham some 4,000 years ago restored blessings, both to him and his descendants, and now is available to anyone in our generation who will enter into it. That's why God's other name is Love. He accepted the life and death of Jesus the Messiah as a substitute for our sin-debt. Now by entering into this covenant, our relationship with the Father is restored and we begin to walk in blessings lost in ancient history.

Many of God's blessings are conditionally based on our obedience rather than being mere gift certificates. "I will bless you *if*. . . (Deuteronomy 28:1, *emphasis mine*). These blessings hover over us and will "overtake us" (28:2) *if* we obey God. As our Creator and Father, He knows what is needed if each one of us is to reach full potential and live joy-filled lives. The Bible is intended as our guide to abundant living, not a rule book of burdensome "thou shalts." Put another way, obeying God brings blessings whereas disobedience unleashes curses. Here's what He says:

> See, I am setting before you today a blessing and a curse—the blessing if you obey the commands of the LORD your God that I am giving you today; the curse if you disobey the commands of the LORD your God.
>
> — DEUTERONOMY 11:26-28

However, there are instances when God blesses and promises to bless simply because He *wants* to bless, not because we have any merit or are required to do something.

Jacob began the struggle with his twin brother in the womb, bargained for the birthright with food, and gained his father's blessing by deception. Yet, through the fascinating interplay between fate and free will, destiny and choice, Jacob still received his parent's blessings and the blessings of God.

> God alone decides which blessings to freely give and which blessings come with a condition.

Only God knows the thoughts and motives of each person. He alone decides which blessings to freely give and which come with a condition.

This call to bless has its roots in the ancient tribe of Levi, who served as priests in their nation "to pronounce blessings in His [God's] name" (Deuteronomy 10:8). Later, Jesus the Messiah expanded this call to bless to include everyone who has been put back right with God, making *every* Christian a priest, invested with the authority and power to bless in Christ's name.

> But you are a chosen people, a royal priesthood,
> a holy nation, a people belonging to God, that
> you may declare the praises of him who called
> you out of darkness into his wonderful light.
> — 1 PETER 2:9

Declaring His praises involves speaking blessings.

Just as Balaam received the command to bless and could not change it (Numbers 23:20), so we have been called to bless because of our God-given ability and authority invested in us through Christ.

Blessing is neither reserved for a special clergy class nor for sacred occasions. Everyone can bless in every situation where blessing is either appropriate or needed.

Gifts for Today

One of the greatest gifts one person can give another is to speak blessings into his or her life. When Rebekah's family sent her away to marry Isaac, they blessed her and said, "Our sister, may you increase to thousands upon thousands; may your offspring possess the gates of their enemies" (Genesis 24:60). With this prophetic blessing, Rebekah became the dynamic person to whom God revealed His plan to work through Jacob rather than Esau. Rebekah set in motion events to see that this plan was properly carried out.

> Blessing is neither reserved for a special clergy class nor for sacred occasions.

Most traditional blessings for people have been given in prayers. Although we might assume the blessings of Aaron in Numbers 6:24-26 and those of Paul in 2 Corinthians 13:14 were prayers, there are no indications these were spoken in that context.

While blessings can be used in prayers, they are more effectively given face-to-face. In prayer blessings, we speak *to* God for the person. In face-to-face blessings, we speak to the person *for* God or on His behalf.

Face-to-face blessings are effective because the face expresses inward thoughts and feelings. Blessing in this way allows us to communicate feelings much better.

In one of our classes, Jim stood behind his seated wife, Marcia, placed his hands on her shoulders, and began speaking wonderful blessings to her. While the words were intimate, the connection was not.

I interrupted and asked Jim to get in front of Marcia, take her hands, look her in the face and continue. Immediately, he saw the greater emotional impact his words had, especially as tears of joy filled her eyes.

> Blessings convey
> God's love to people.

When Jacob was re-united with his brother Esau after twenty years, they embraced and wept together. Jacob looked in his brother's face and said, "For to see your face is like seeing the face of God" (Genesis 33:10).

WHY WE SHOULD BLESS

One of the main purposes of blessing is to convey the love of Father God to someone. Peter tells us "this is what you are called to do" (1 Peter 3:9). Through blessing, God's love and affirmations are spoken into a person's life.

When a blessing is received and accepted, many things happen. I've seen people repent, break free from evil torment, begin their walk with God, and experience emotional as well as physical healing—either instantly or gradually. In several cases, marriages have been healed as one spouse spoke blessings upon the other, expressing dormant thoughts and feelings.

Such was the case when we met Charles Bevel and his wife, Ramona, during a weekend seminar. Charles seemed very cordial and friendly. Ramona, however, sat down near a corner, arms crossed, and stared at the far end of the room. In our first session everyone tried to ignore her. Everyone but Charles, who struggled to conceal his embarrassment.

Near the end of the evening, I demonstrated the power of blessing as I took my wife's hands, looked her in the eyes, and told her how much fun it was living with her. After affirming her as a wife, mother, and grandmother, I assured her of my love and commitment to her for the rest of our lives.

She returned the blessing in such a moving way, several handkerchiefs appeared.

"Does someone else have a blessing to give?" I asked.

Charles was up on his feet, heading to the back corner before I barely finished the question. He pulled a chair up in front of Ramona, put his hand under her chin and slowly raised her head until their eyes met.

"Ramona," he said, "I've been a fool to withhold my blessings from you and our three children. I know that I haven't been there for you like I should. Working long hours is no excuse for my neglect. Please forgive me.

"Honey, I bless you for being such a wonderful wife and mother. And cook? You make better biscuits than my mother.

"I recommit my life and love to you tonight. I promise to make time for you and the children and be by your side for as long as I live."

By this time, tears were running down Ramona's cheeks. After a long pause, she said, "Charles, I had no idea that you felt that way. Why didn't you *tell* me that you love and appreciate me? All these years, I've been longing to be the kind of wife you need."

During our last seminar session, members of the group bought a wedding cake and bouquet for Ramona and Charles, who renewed their marriage vows before everyone.

HOW BLESSING WORKS

Blessing not only conveys God's love, but imparts His favor as well. As Aaron spoke the divine name over the people, God said He would be present *in* the blessing to impart blessings to them (Numbers 6:22-27). This blessing contained protection ("The Lord bless you and keep you"), special favor, ("The Lord make His face to shine on you"), power and peace ("The Lord lift up His countenance on you and give you peace"). As amazing as it sounds, this spoken blessing actually put God's name on people ("So they will put my name on the Israelites, and I will bless them"), releasing the Spirit of God in their lives.

> There is a natural, inner hunger we all share, a need to be blessed.

Through parents, blessings impart life to children who receive them. Parents who bless their children on a regular basis can expect very positive results because blessings build God's character and activate God's covenant promises in their lives.

> He redeemed us in order that the blessing given to Abraham might come to the Gentiles through Christ Jesus, so that by faith we might receive the promise of the Spirit.
> — GALATIANS 3:14

As powerful as blessing is, there is no guarantee that God's presence will be received. Judas rejected the blessings of Jesus. Absalom rejected his father's blessings as well.

Blessings, however, aren't easily brushed off. That's because there is a natural, inner hunger we share, a need to be blessed.

After one of our seminars, a father gathered his family around the Friday night dinner table to talk about blessings and to bless each member of his family. All went well until his teenage son, Tim, complained that he was bored and wanted to leave the table and watch television.

Nevertheless, Tim's father put his hands on his son's head, looked him in the eyes, and told him how proud he was to have him for a son. Quoting Isaiah 11:2, he said:

> May you be as Ephraim and Manasseh who were doubly blessed. May the Spirit of the LORD rest on you—the Spirit of wisdom and of understanding, the Spirit of counsel and of power, the Spirit of knowledge and of the fear of the LORD.

Tim successfully masked any positive response to the whole evening, including this blessing.

Yet on Friday morning of the following week during breakfast, Tim asked his dad, "Dad, I like that blessing stuff. Are we going to do it again tonight?"

While this teenage reaction might be atypical, it points to the deep hunger we all have for blessings. Because we are created by the God whose nature is to bless, that need is in our emotional blueprint or DNA.

VEHICLE OF BLESSING

The Bible frequently records and demonstrates how words convey messages, either positive or negative. Proverbs, in particular, contains admonitions to use words wisely.

> With his mouth the godless destroys his neigh-
> bor, but through knowledge the righteous
> escape (11:9).

> Reckless words pierce like a sword, but the
> tongue of the wise brings healing (12:18).

> The tongue that brings healing is the tree of life,
> but a deceitful tongue crushes the spirit (15:4).

> The tongue has the power of life and death, and
> those who love it will eat its fruit (18:21).

The Book of James uses vivid imagery to emphasize the
way words affect people and situations, either for good or for
evil. He likens the tongue to a horse's bridle or the rudder of
a ship.

> When we put bits into the mouths of horses to
> make them obey us, we can turn the whole ani-
> mal. Or take ships as an example. Although they
> are so large and are driven by strong winds, they
> are steered by a very small rudder wherever the
> pilot wants to go. Likewise the tongue is a small
> part of the body, but it makes great boasts.
> — JAMES 3:3-5

Words charged with such potential power can initiate
either a curse or a blessing, as amply demonstrated by Jesus
years ago. Storms, fig trees, demons, and dead people
responded to His voice.

To encourage us to exercise faith and use divine authority available through Him, Jesus challenged us with the art of mountain moving.

> I tell you the truth, if anyone says to this mountain, "Go, throw yourself into the sea," and does not doubt in his heart but believes that what he says will happen, it will be done for him.
>
> — MARK 11:23

Was He speaking figuratively or making a literal reference to the power of faith released by words? Recall the time when His words to a fig tree brought instant results (Matthew 21:19), or later, when Peter said to a lame beggar, "In the name of Jesus Christ of Nazareth, walk." Instantly the man's ankles and feet became strong as he jumped to his feet and began to walk (Acts 3:8).

Blessings, flowing from the fountainhead of God, need a delivery vehicle, a communication method whereby benefits can be received and understood. Words are such vehicles because they carry:

- creative power
- seeds
- thoughts and feelings
- messages.

Words Carry Creative Power

God created the universe by speaking it into existence. Seven times He said, "Let there be..." and there was! *This ability to speak things into existence is how we are like God.* Far from being magical, words do create good or bad, life or death.

Bill Glass, author of *Expect To Win*, tells of the occasion when a mother introduced her children to him.

> "This is my little girl. She's very timid." And the little girl stood with her finger in her mouth.
> "This is my little boy. He's a bully." Sure enough, there he stood with chest out, muscles flexed, frowning like a bulldog.
> "This is my other little boy. He's very dumb." There he stood with a dumb look on his face.

Those children were becoming creations of their mother's words. Since life and death are in the power of the tongue, we are told to speak life that creates good character, self-worth, and a noble destiny in our children and grandchildren, as well as people around us. We'll see in a moment that we are called to even bless troublesome or irregular people in our lives.

Our ability to speak things into existence is how we are like God.

Springtime was an important time on the farm where I grew up. During the planting season, getting the first row straight in the field was a big thing, especially for my Dad. He would go to the other end of the field and tie his white handkerchief on a fence post as a flag. "Just keep your eye on the flag," he would tell us. "You can plow a straight row if you keep your eye on the flag."

Words too, like a flag in the distance, can help guide us toward becoming a better person.

Words Carry Seeds

Seeds produce after their kind; you can't get a pine tree from an acorn. Words produce in like manner, often having a noticeable impact on a person—immediately visible at times, slowly sprouting at other times.

Ron Wallace discovered this after attending our seminar on blessing. With a heightened awareness of the power of words, the next day he shouted to a grumpy mail carrier pulling away from his mail box, "God bless you today!"

Suddenly, the truck came to an abrupt halt, then backed up. "What did you say to me?" he asked.

"I said, 'God bless you today.'"

The mail carrier's disposition visibly changed. He smiled and said, "Thank you."

> Pharaoh's last words to Moses were, "Bless me before you go."

On a larger scale, one can see the effects of these word-seeds in the negotiations for the release of Hebrew slaves in Egypt. While the biblical record doesn't record all that was said between Moses and Pharaoh, one remarkable request by the Egyptian king is recorded. "Go! And also bless me" (Exodus 12:32). It seems Moses' words had finally taken root.

Words Carry Thoughts and Feelings

Spoken words reveal feelings, opinions, and facts, even clothed in the laughter of joke-jabbing. Strip away the laughter and you'll hear what is *actually* being said. Matthew wrote: "Out of the overflow of the heart the mouth speaks" (12:34). Words also reveal feelings of admiration and affirmation. In a recent marriage enrichment group, Harry took his wife's hand, looked her in the eyes and said, "Harriet, you are the most important person in my life. Thank you for being such a good mother and wife. If I had searched the whole world, I would not have found a woman that thrills me like you do."

Harriet replied, "That's the first time in years you've looked into my eyes and told me how you felt. Thank you."

Words Carry Messages

A friend of mine told the story of one of her childhood playmates named Bobby. Over the years he became rebellious as anger, bitterness, and resentment took root in his life—against God, his parents, and his church. His life became consumed with drugs as he gradually became shackled with addictions.

One day Bobby disappeared. His brokenhearted parents didn't know if he killed himself with an overdose or was murdered by a drug gang. For two years they didn't hear anything from their son, not one phone call, card, or letter.

He simply vanished.

Then one day Bobby's dad felt the crushing grip of months of pent-up frustration and pain while driving on the outskirts of the city where he lived. He pulled his car off on the side of the road, got out and walked off some distance from the highway. He pointed his finger towards the north and yelled with all his might, "BOBBY, COME HOME!" Turning to the south, he shouted in the wind, "BOBBY,

COME HOME!" To the east and west, same words.

Two days later, this dad heard a knock at the door. There stood Bobby.

Bobby was home.

It didn't take long before his dad asked, "Son, what brought you home?"

"Dad, . . ." Bobby said, ". . . I was sitting on the front porch of an old shack on the edge of the desert in Arizona, stoned out of my mind. A wind started blowing and suddenly grew stronger. Dad, I could have sworn that I heard your voice in the wind, BOBBY, COME HOME! And, Dad, I got here just as fast as I could."

And so another prodigal son finally makes it home!

Words *are* containers, having "the power of life and death" (Proverbs 18:21). You have this power within you, the authority and right to speak in line with God's word. Take advantage of it!

WHAT BLESSING BRINGS

How should someone react to insults or hurtful words hurled their way? In the pagan, hostile society of Peter's day, the common response to hostility was retaliation, but Peter admonished his readers: *Never pay back one wrong with another, or an angry word with another one; instead, pay back with a blessing. This is what you are called to do, so that you inherit a blessing yourself.*

> Spoken blessings have the power to change the atmosphere around us.

A gracious response can take the edge off of hurtful words and stop shock waves of animosities. In short, spoken blessings stem anger. Rather than reacting to anger with anger, we can choose to speak words of blessing.

But most of the time we find ourselves in situations where no one is upset or angry. Someone just needs blessing. They need the gift we can give by speaking positive words into their lives.

As we make blessing part of our lifestyle, blessings begin to come back to us. As we bless, we are blessed because we speak in line with our Father God who blesses and calls us to this lifestyle. Spoken blessings have the power to change people and the atmosphere around us. They:

- reverse curses
- curb anger and resentment
- give expression to friendship and goodwill.

Most remarkably, as we speak blessings to other people, God's storehouse of "welfare, happiness, and protection (1 Peter 3:9, *The Amplified Bible*) is released in their lives—and ours!

Blessing of welfare

Someone who "fares well" is not shaken by adverse circumstances. He or she experiences a general sense of well-being, often described in terms of material prosperity.

> Land that drinks in the rain often falling on it
> and that produces a crop useful to those for
> whom it is farmed receives the blessing of God.
> — HEBREWS 6:7

Blessings of welfare extend far beyond material benefits. This well-being is more internal than external. It's about who a person is more than what he has. It's about abiding joy more than momentary pleasure. Welfare is the blessing that comes as someone embraces God's goodness and learns to walk with Him.

A good example of many people experiencing God's favor can be seen in India, where thirty-five percent of a population of one billion people live in poverty. Many new Christians live in the context of open hostility and rejection from family and fellow villagers, yet their living standard rises dramatically once they are converted, even if wages are a meager two dollars a day. Why? First, they are delivered from their costly addictions. Second, most experience some kind of divine healing which makes expensive trips to the witch doctor unnecessary. Third, they stop borrowing money (for addictions and for witch doctors) from local loan sharks charging exorbitant rates.

Blessing of Happiness and Favor

Everyone wants to be happy—from Sleeping Beauty to the Hunchback of Notre Dame. But happiness is often skewed by the pursuit of money, popularity, good looks, or possessions, none of which guarantee the blessing of happiness. Howard Hughes comes to mind. Although notably one of the richest men on earth, he died a deeply disturbed, lonely recluse.

While happiness is contained in the idea of welfare or well-being, it is about attitude or mood more than circumstances. In the New Testament, Paul and Silas were happy even in a filthy dungeon. Their inner state was not entirely dependent upon their external circumstances.

God *is* concerned about our happiness—so much so that He sent His Son to earth years ago to restore our broken relationships and teach us how to be happy by learning to walk with God and one another. Our daily walks, attitudes, and moods change because life's important questions are answered:

> God is concerned about our happiness.

- What is life all about?
  Perhaps it's more about others and less about me.
- Why am I alive?
  Perhaps to bring honor to God with my life and develop my walk with Him.
- What is really important?
  Perhaps to develop my inner self and serve other people.

God's concern for our happiness and well-being was underscored as my wife and I changed planes in Newark on the way to Israel. I checked in with a ticket agent named Nora and asked if our assigned seats could be replaced with ones nearer the front of the aircraft for the nine-hour flight to Tel Aviv.

"Be glad you have seats," she said. "We have overbooked this flight and many people are flying standby."

Satisfied to have assigned seats, we walked out into the concourse to await our boarding call some thirty minutes later.

As the crowd began to move toward the boarding gate, I glanced over at Nora. She was making a hand motion that I thought was for someone standing next to us. A moment later, I saw Nora looking directly at me, motioning for me to come to her counter.

"Give me your tickets," she said. "Tonight, you're riding in my cabin." I didn't have a clue what she was talking about, but handed her our two tickets. After a few moments on her computer, she looked at us and said, "Follow me and don't let me lose you in the crowd. I have to get you past the gate."

Nora began weaving through awaiting passengers, ducking under ropes, passing agents at the boarding gate, and finally down to the door of the aircraft with us in tow. "Stand here until I get you two seats together," she said.

To my amazement, we were standing just inside the first-class cabin. Surely she has made a mistake. She must think we are someone else. What in the world is this all about?

After Nora played musical chairs with three other passengers, she came back to us. "I have two seats in the middle. I hope that's okay with you," she said.

It isn't easy to describe an overwhelming feeling, but I sat quietly as the Lord's presence seemed to fill the cabin. In a moment, He spoke to my inner self:

You didn't do one thing to deserve this. I did this to show you my love.

I know, Father.

What aircraft did I put you on? He gently spoke.

It's a 777. (Seven is the biblical number for completion.)

Yes, I have completed a major work in your life. And what row have I put you on?

I looked up under the overhead bins. *Row eight.* (The number for new beginnings.)

Yes, I'm beginning a new work in you.

That night I learned anew the meaning of undeserved love and favor. There is a Father who wants to show favor to His children.

Blessing of Protection

Divine protection, or lack of it, is viewed according to a person's perspective of life, God, and the Bible. Many non-believers, as well as some Christians, discount any divine intervention in their daily lives. They say either there is no God at all or He does not intervene in human affairs today.

However, I believe the Bible is not only true but is a reliable guide for anyone who chooses to walk with God. Events recounted in the biblical record continue to occur today, especially in regard to God's divine protection.

Ray from the Bhil Tribe in India is a case in point. Before the Gospel came to his remote region, Ray sacrificed goats to stone gods and made his living as a roadside robber. Christ arrested him and empowered him as a zealous church planter and overseer of twenty-five house churches.

On the last day of our Indore, India, seminar, Ray came through the line to say goodbye. As I embraced him for the last time, the word of the Lord came to me. *Speak a blessing of protection over him.*

I did.

Two weeks later, Ray and two friends were preaching the Gospel in a remote village. Tribesmen with bows and arrows ambushed them. All three sustained wounds, one seriously. Ray suffered only a slight flesh wound under his right arm.

Even after the attack, Ray and his friends have repeatedly returned to the village, not only preaching, but publicly forgiving and blessing their attackers. Results? Many villagers have become followers of the Prince of Peace.

One of God's methods of protection is expressed through angels—mentioned nearly three hundred times in the Bible. Not only do these holy deputies carry out God's will on earth, but they often protect people from danger and death. *Joel News International* reported that on January 20, 1999, several Christian young people in Indonesia were hacked to death by Muslim radicals. When one youth escaped into the jungle, a young girl dressed in white met him. She took him to safety in the village of Hatiwe Besar and disappeared. Simply vanished!

One of God's methods of protection is expressed through angels.

These "powerful angels" (2 Thessalonians 1:7) "guard you in all your ways" (Psalm 91:11). Billy Graham's book, *Angels: God's Secret Agents*, recounts many instances where God's protection came through angels. A good biblical example is the time an angel freed Peter from prison where he was awaiting death.

> So Peter was kept in prison, but the church was earnestly praying to God for him.
>
> The night before Herod was to bring him to trial, Peter was sleeping between two soldiers, bound with two chains, and sentries stood guard at the entrance. Suddenly an angel of the Lord appeared and a light shone in the cell. He struck Peter on the side and woke him up, "Quick, get up!" he said, and the chains fell off Peter's wrists.
>
> Then the angel said to him, "Put on your clothes and sandals." And Peter did so. "Wrap your cloak around you and follow me," the angel told him. Peter followed him out of the prison, but he had no idea that what the angel was doing was really happening; he thought he was seeing a vision. They passed the first and

second guards and came to the iron gate leading
to the city. It opened for them by itself, and they
went through it. When they had walked the
length of one street, suddenly, the angel left him.

— ACTS 12:5-10

Any discussion about God's protection quickly raises the
question, "But how do you explain times when a person was
not protected?"

I can't.

Hebrews 11 addressed this issue in what someone has
called, "God's Hall of Fame"—saints who suffered, were
imprisoned, tortured, and killed. Why? Because God has a
mysterious plan to allow some people to suffer and die *by
faith*. Billy Graham wrote in the above-mentioned book:
"The latter part of Hebrews 11 indicates that those who
received no visible help in answer to prayer will have a far
greater heavenly reward because they endured by faith
alone."

SPEAK TO THE FOUNTAINHEAD

When the two-man commando unit of Moses and Aaron
liberated the Egyptian labor camps, they took an evacuation
route through an arid desert. Amid anarchic uproar, God
instructed Moses to speak to a rock so sufficient water would
flow to quench thirsty people and livestock.

Simple. Just *speak* to the rock.

However, amid collective rebellion and strife, Moses hes-
itated to speak in faith to the fountainhead (not believing
what God told him would occur). Instead, he struck the rock
twice with his staff, dishonoring God and His words before

the people. Consequently, Moses' inheritance of promised land was lost through silence (disobedience).

Now, years later, you may find yourself in dry places of need or want. "Speak to that rock . . . and it will pour out its water" (Numbers 20:8). I'm suggesting a fountain of blessing is released as you walk with God and speak faith-filled words. Begin by speaking to (and walking with) the Fountainhead to possess your inheritance *now*.

THREE

POSSESS YOUR
INHERITANCE *NOW*

INHERITING BLESSINGS is one thing. Possessing blessings is quite another—as I learned years ago.

"Hello, Dr. Reddick, this is Cliff Walters. Could we meet for coffee?" the voice on the phone asked.

After a few minutes of get-to-know-you conversation in a local cafe, he handed me a folded check. "I'm not part of your congregation, but I understand you need books for your personal library," he said.

Picture the shock on my twenty-something-year-old face as I opened it and read the amount—out loud, "$10,000!" (To put this in perspective, that would be about $40,000 today.)

"Since these books will help make you a better teacher and pastor, I made the check out to your church. I'm sure that won't be a problem."

It was.

When I mentioned the check to the church finance chairman, he thought that much money from someone outside the congregation would likely raise jealousy and cause misunderstanding in the church. His reaction to the check caught me off-guard.

For three agonizing weeks, I carried the check in my pocket, occasionally unfolding it for yet another look at the amount. Questions interrupted my concentration and sleep. Stir up jealousy? Agitate the congregation? Is he sure? Does he realize how many books and ministry resources that much money will buy?

> Having something is not the same as possessing it.

Finally, I decided what to do with the $10,000 check.

A phone call arranged a second meeting with Mr. Walters. I briefly explained the objections raised and slowly handed him the well-worn check. "Thank you for your trust and generosity," I said. "But I can't accept it and run the risk of upsetting people in the church."

That experience taught me the vast difference between merely obtaining and actually possessing. Peter stressed this difference when he wrote: "so that you will inherit a blessing yourself." The Greek word he used for inherit means *"to obtain by possessing."*

This chapter is about you inheriting many blessings—and possessing them—*now* rather than later or in the sweet by-and-by.

POSSESSING YOUR BLESSINGS

In most Western cultures, inheritance is usually received after someone's death. This bittersweet custom has a few negative implications, one of which can be an heir's subtle or even subconscious death wish for a parent or insured spouse. The effects of death can have a Cinderella effect, instantly transforming an heir from want to wealth, poverty to plenty, obscurity to prominence. Death can be like an heir hitting the jackpot!

In Middle-Eastern biblical culture, there were two ways to distribute property and wealth from parents to children, especially sons. This was done by a will after death, as in the West, or by a gift while the benefactor was living. Both methods are present in the Bible, but the most prominent manner in which an inheritance passed to sons was by a gift *while the father was alive*, portrayed in the story of the two sons in Luke 15.

"Father, give me my share of the estate," the younger son demanded. So the father's property was "divided" (v.31) between the two boys and the younger set off on his extravagant binge.

The prodigal son's gallivanting led to debauchery and, finally, a pigpen. After some time he came to his senses and started home. At least he could be one of his father's hired servants, he thought.

What awaited him was not rebuke and servitude but restoration as part of the family—complete with shoes, signet ring, and robe. His identity and destiny were graciously restored by a loving father.

The unfolding events of this saga encapsulate the gospel within the Gospels. They focus on the steadfast love of a father who welcomed back a returning, repentant son. Imagine the son's surprise when his father made him the guest of honor at his homecoming banquet.

STOREHOUSE OF GIFTS

The story of the wandering prodigal who returned to a loving, forgiving father is a story that describes with touching simplicity what God is like—good, gracious, merciful, and loving—eager for everyone to have their relationship restored with Him.

Jesus the Messiah did exactly that for everyone embracing what He did—taking upon Himself our sins and judgment penalties through His agony and death in Jerusalem years ago. The very thing severed was restored.

> The Holy Spirit gives us God's mind, character and power.

As we repent (change mind and direction) and return to Father God, He sends His Spirit to live in us (Romans 8:9). This divine impregnation is the supreme gift of His personhood. In other words, we receive His mind (1 Corinthians 2:16), His character (2 Peter 1:4), and His power (Acts 1:8) that become a kind of onboard internal navigation system. We'll know where to walk, which way to turn, and how to get Home.

There's more good news.

While all these blessings are for us now, as we receive this new kind of (eternal) life through Jesus Christ, our Father does reserve a final blessing after we die. We are invited to live in His House forever (John 14)!

Jesus opened the door for us to receive spiritual gifts, both then (Acts 2) and now (1 Peter 4:10). These gifts are just that—gifts for today, not only after someone dies. In fact, someone did die that we might inherit our Father's bounty now rather than just in the hereafter. The Kingdom (rulership) of God is *now,* Jesus told the inquirers sent by John the Baptizer.

> "Go and tell John the things you have seen and heard: that the blind see, the lame walk, the lepers are cleansed, the deaf hear, the dead are raised, the poor have the gospel preached to them."
>
> — JOHN 7:22

Paul expanded participation in the Kingdom of God to include *every* Christian because "you were washed, you were sanctified, you were justified in the name of the Lord Jesus Christ and by the Spirit of our God" (1 Corinthians 6:11).

The land of Canaan was Israel's inheritance, but they had to possess it through work and war, faith and fight (Deuteronomy 4:20). Our storehouse of blessings is available, but we must *possess* blessings by learning to walk with God, learning to listen and obey what we hear Him say. By doing this, not only do our wants change, but our hearts do also.

> Our storehouse of blessings becomes available once we begin listening to God and obeying what He says.

WELLSPRING OF LIFE

The biblical writers used "heart" as a metaphor for wellspring or source of a person's life. It refers to one's inner self—the control center of thinking and ethical living. This is why Peter urged us to make Christ ruler in our heart since the heart is who we are.

> But in your hearts set apart Christ as Lord.
> Always be prepared to give an answer to everyone
> who asks you to give the reasons for the hope that
> you have. But do this with gentleness and respect.
> — 1 PETER 3:15

Guarding this wellspring of life is necessary due to our fallen nature of self-centered impulses and unmet needs.

But how? Can we guard our inner self by sheer determination and strong will?

Absolutely not, according to Peter! We are shielded only by God's power as we believe He is able to keep us from falling into our lower impulses. Divine power comes where human faith opens the door and asks for help.

> Divine power comes where human faith opens the door and asks for help.

So as Christ becomes the ruler of your heart or life, you receive His character, mind, and power. All are part of your inheritance. Your faith in Christ and obedience to His voice open the Father's storehouse of blessings, "for the eyes of the LORD are on the righteous, and his ears are attentive to their prayer" (1 Peter 3:12).

3 KEYS YOU NEED

God gave the Israelites the region of Canaan in the Middle-East as an inheritance. A scouting party concluded that the country was rich in natural resources but was inhabited by giants. "Do not go there!" was the majority report that was accepted by the Israeli leadership. Because of their fear and lack of faith, God caused Israel to wander aimlessly in the desert region for forty years.

Now, a full generation later, some two million people were poised on the eastern side of the Jordan River, ready to move into the land promised by God as their inheritance— an inheritance that they could possess *now.* To believe this blessing was from God wasn't enough. They had to act on it. God's part was to give; their part was to take the land.

This age-old principle of faith (believing a promise) and effort (acting on the promise) is relevant for us today.

The Hebrew word, bless (*barak*) paints a graphic word picture of a camel kneeling to eat and rest. While in this position the camel can be loaded with cargo—goods that will bless other people. Likewise, as you rest in God's promises (some 8,000 promises are in the Bible), you are loaded with blessings as you learn to hear Him speak specific blessings (*rhema* words) for you and other people.

There are three keys you can use to unlock your inheritance of blessings now: forgive and bless, ask, then expect.

Forgive and Bless

The first key that unlocks the divine storehouse and releases your blessings is forgiveness combined with blessing. Jesus said, "But I tell you who hear me: Love your enemies, do good to those who hate you, bless those who curse you, pray for those who mistreat you" (Luke 6:27-28). This process of forgiving involves loving, doing good, blessing, and praying. Forgive *and* bless. Unless an attitude of forgiving and blessing is deeply rooted in a person's life, God's blessings are hindered or blocked.

Ask

The second key to your God-given inheritance is simply *asking* for blessings.

Remember Jabez?

> "Oh, that You would bless me indeed, and enlarge my territory, that Your hand would be with me, and that You would keep me from evil, that I may not cause pain!" So God granted him what he requested.
> — 1 CHRONICLES 4:10, *New King James Version*

Sound over-simplistic? Unrealistic?

Asking for specific blessings acknowledges God as your Source as well as your dependence on Him. Far from casually uttered words that might hit the divine jackpot, God delights in blessing those who walk with Him daily—a restored walk made possible by Jesus Christ.

The Amplified Bible captures the meaning of *ask* in the Greek text. "Keep on asking and it will be given you; keep on seeking and you will find; keep on knocking [reverently] and the door will be opened to you" (Matthew 7:7). The Gospel writer concludes this thought by quoting Jesus.

> If you, then, evil as you are, know how to give good and advantageous gifts to your children, how much more will your Father Who is in heaven [perfect as He is] give good and advantageous things to those who keep on asking Him!
> — MATTHEW 7:11

Go ahead. Ask for God's blessings!

Expect

The third key to God's storehouse of blessings is your *expectancy* or faith. His blessings come to you on two tracks similar to those of a railroad. One is prayer (conversation with God); the other is faith (expecting results as you ask). For example, two blind men came to Jesus for healing. "According to your faith will it be done to you," He said. Their sight was immediately restored!

> Faith is drawing a mental picture of the blessing completed.

However, there were occasions when lack of faith greatly hindered the power of Jesus.

> Jesus said to them, "Only in his hometown, among his relatives and in his own house is a prophet without honor." He could not do any miracles there, except lay his hands on a few sick people and heal them. And he was amazed at their lack of faith.
>
> — MARK 6:4-6

Isaac added faith to his blessings for Jacob and Esau. So did Joseph when he blessed his twelve sons and two grandsons. These two men are listed in Hebrews as examples of faith (11:20-21) because their blessings contained faith to help shape their children's lives.

Faith for Saints

When we think of faith, past spiritual giants come to mind; saints who either looked weird, talked funny, walked on water, or lived in monasteries. These mythic superheros leaped over tall buildings in a single bound and raised the dead with a single word. Their faith seemed to rush out of nowhere and triumph in every situation.

What is this faith needed for blessing? Is it a mysterious unction of the past or mystical ointment for the present? Does it transform common sinners into elite saints?

> Miracles always occur in the field of faith.

Hebrews gives a good definition. Faith is "being sure of what we hope for and do not see" (Hebrews 11:1). Faith is *seeing* what is still incubating; *calling forth* what is still in the process; *accepting* what is still on the potter's wheel; *believing* as future what is still present.

Faith is drawing a mental picture of the blessing completed. Rather than superstitious voodoo or mind control, this is blessing from deep impressions about the person or situation. Faith is holding firm a mental picture.

A woman repeatedly complained about her husband's lack of spiritual interest. Even after praying for years, she saw no encouraging signs. "Why hasn't Ben changed?" she asked.

I asked her a question in response. "Can you imagine Ben on fire for God, praying with you, and blessing you? Can you see Ben this way?"

"Of course not!" she said.

"Maybe that's why he isn't," I replied.

As we "see" the blessing fulfilled, our blessing and faith help provide the tracks on which God's power travels. Jesus said to a woman instantly healed, "Your faith has healed you" (Matthew 9:22).

Miracles always occur in the field of faith, the supernatural realm beyond our reason or logic.

Faith for Sinners

What chance do you have to tap this kind of faith and mix with blessing? Two jobs and several children may not leave time even for church. Or, perhaps you've either given up on the religious stuff or never had much interest in spiritual things.

Where does blessing fit into the life of a "non-religious" person? Is this a God-thing for saints only, a goody two-shoes exercise?

God can use anyone—religious or not—to impart blessings because of:

1. the nature of words
2. a person's natural abilities
3. everyone's innate hunger for blessings.

Nowhere is this principle more clearly demonstrated than in the case of Balaam. Although his spiritual state was described as "wicked" (2 Peter 2:15), his blessings for the Israelites still had a powerful effect.

1. The nature of words

Already, we've seen that words are like seeds and vehicles: they produce after their kind and carry messages, thoughts, and feelings from one person to another. Furthermore, words can create either good or evil in their wake, setting in motion blessing or cursing.

2. Natural abilities

Faith is "being sure of what we hope for and do not see." A crucial element of faith is seeing something in the mind and believing it will happen beforehand. All of us have this God-given ability because everyone is created in the image or likeness of God.

> So God created man in his own image, in the
> image of God he created him; male and female
> he created them.
>
> — GENESIS 1:27

Even an unbeliever, often referred to as "Gentile" in the New Testament, has a God-consciousness and an inner faith to believe things that are not visible.

> When Gentiles who have not [the divine] Law
> do instinctively what the Law requires ... they
> show that the essential requirements of the Law
> are written in their hearts and are operating
> there...
>
> — ROMANS 2:14-15, *The Amplified Bible*

Thus, anyone can hope for the unseen and hold a picture in mind until it comes to pass. This hope is combined with blessings that flow from one's natural abilities due to the divine imprint in every person.

Because of this Creator-creature connection, everyone can bless by expressing love, kindness, and affirmations that enrich another person's life.

Everyone can bless by expressing love, kindness, and affirmations that enrich another's life.

A Christian, however, has a decided advantage over the unbeliever in this regard because, whereas the latter is trying to focus his or her individual mind on an outcome, the Christian is tapped into and bringing to bear on the situation the power of God! Drawing strength and support from a power both within and outside ourselves is extremely important in matters of faith.

The issue is not one's ability. It's usually our lack of practice. I like one man's advice to a friend: "Try blessing your wife, even if it frightens her at first."

3. Innate hunger for blessings

This God-man link not only gives everyone the ability to bless, but accounts for everyone's hunger *for* blessings. Humans are three-part beings: spirit, soul, and body. Every part of our triune nature craves blessings—human and divine.

BEGIN NOW!

To know you can start receiving blessings today is one thing. Receiving them is another. But, the journey of a thousand miles begins with the first step. Take that step right now. Ask the Lord to forgive you of any unforgiveness you have harbored in the past. Sitting right where you are, ask God to bless and show favor to any bothersome person you know. This clears the way for your divine blessings.

Now, ask that your storehouse doors be opened and your blessings begin to flow. Expect to see your Heavenly Father move on your behalf as you walk with Him daily. This walk is one of talking, listening, and obeying what you hear. You are moving from unforgiveness into forgiveness, from hurt into healing, from fear into faith, and from curses into blessings.

You are becoming a new person in Christ. Your lifestyle is changing!

FOUR

YOUR NEW LIFESTYLE

IN A LATE AFTERNOON WORKSHOP, I asked if anyone had blessings for someone in the group. Tom Farrar quickly turned to his wife, Nelda, and said, "I want to do something I have never done during the forty years we've been married. You know that I wasn't raised this way, but I'm going to bless you if it kills me."

Tom struggled as love and admiration for Nelda slowly surfaced in his blessing. He continued to affirm her for some ten minutes.

"From this day on," he assured her, "I'll bless you *every* day for the rest of our lives."

"Tom, that's the best news I've heard in years!" Nelda said.

Tom and Nelda were among the last to leave the room, but not before he said to me, "This has been the most significant day of my life."

"Nelda," I said, looking at Tom, "Every time I see you, I am going to ask if he is still blessing you."

A few months later the couple registered for a three-day

camp we conducted near Chicago. Across the campus, I rec-
ognized Tom and shouted a hello, but wasn't sure who the
woman was with Him. It didn't look like Nelda. I wondered
what happened.

"The difference between a princess and a flower girl is how she is treated."

Quickly, I walked toward
them, still puzzled about this
unfamiliar woman with him.
After greeting Tom, I said, "Is
that you, Nelda?"

It was.

I could hardly believe daily blessings had changed her
looks that much!

One is reminded of Eliza Doolittle's comment in the
Broadway musical, *My Fair Lady*: "The difference between a
princess and a flower girl is how she is treated."

12 TIMES THAT A BLESSING IS NEEDED MOST

As you begin to mix faith with blessing, your lifestyle
changes. With that comes a new awareness of times when
other people seem to need or want blessing. Wave after wave
of encouragement and affirmation for other people flow
from your storehouse of abundant blessings.

Tom discovered that *anytime* is a good time to bless
Nelda. However, there are specific times blessings can especially release God's power, goodness, favor, and protection in
someone's life.

1. Conception and Pregnancy

An unborn child's ability to receive messages and stimuli
outside the womb has been documented by modern

research. The Bible also notes this in Elizabeth's words to Mary. "As soon as the sound of your greetings reached my ears, the baby in my womb leaped for joy" (Luke 1:44). Spoken blessings begin to shape the child's identity and destiny even in the womb. Also, they can be appropriately spoken over parents-to-be.

Jeremiah is an example of the power that blessings had even before he was born. God said to Jeremiah, "Before I formed you in the womb I knew you, before you were born I set you apart; I appointed you as a prophet to the nations" (Jeremiah. 1:5). If God blessed unborn Jeremiah with an anointing, we would do well to follow His example by frequently blessing unborn children.

I had an opportunity to exercise such a blessing when our daughter became pregnant. The first few months of the pregnancy went as we all hoped: full of excitement and positive test results. Then, in the sixth month, Laura went into labor. This crisis forced her onto hospital bedrest for the next three months.

In response to a phone call one afternoon, my wife and I quickly drove to the hospital. Many troubling questions came to mind. Is Laura on the verge of a miscarriage? Is she going to have a premature child? Is this a physical or spiritual battle we're facing? Or both?

Seated around the hospital bed among the gathering of her husband and friends, my mind kept going back to the words of Jesus:

> Have faith in God. I tell you the truth, if anyone says to this mountain, "Go throw yourself into the sea," and does not doubt in his heart but believes that what he says will happen, it will be done for him.
> — MARK 11:22-23

Why couldn't that authority be used with our unborn granddaughter? I wondered.

Before long a lull came in the conversation and something welled up within me. I moved closer to the bed and placed my hand on Laura's stomach and spoke to the child in her womb: "Honey, this is your Papa. Don't come out yet. It's not time." I paused. Stillness had settled in the room. I felt a strong sense of peace settling over me as well. I leaned in closer yet, and spoke the words again; "This is Papa. Don't come out yet. Now is not the time."

I continued this one-sided conversation with our granddaughter until the thirty-seventh week when Kayla came out of the womb, a healthy six pounds, six ounces!

——— #1 IDENTITY ———

Blessing shapes
who we are.

---

2. Birth/Birthdays

The angel Gabriel said that John the Baptizer would be filled with the Holy Spirit "even from birth" (Luke 1:15). When he was born, relatives and neighbors gathered to "magnify" the Lord (Luke 1:58, *The Nestle Greek Text*) and rejoice together. Blessings are clearly inferred in praising God and rejoicing with parents.

Similarly, Paul's testimony of early blessings included his gratitude that God "set me apart from birth and called me by his grace" (Galatians 1:15).

Minutes after our grandson was born, I held him in my arms and said this blessing: *"Ethan, I'm so proud you're in our*

bers help ease the adjustment to school, work, or living con-
ditions. Blessing gives confidence, encouragement, and "you-
can-do-it" assurance.

Before Jacob left his father's house, Isaac spoke a farewell
blessing over him even though Jacob had deceived him
(Genesis 28:3-4):

> May God Almighty bless you and make you
> fruitful and increase your numbers until you
> become a community of peoples. May he give
> you and your descendants the blessing given to
> Abraham, so that you may take possession of the
> land where you now live as an alien, the land
> God gave to Abraham.
>
> — GENESIS 28:3-4

―――― #6 CONFIDENCE ――――

Blessing gives

"You-can-do-it!"

assurance.

7. Marriage

We hear blessings during wedding festivities more frequently than other times. These expressions of health, happiness, and long life vary from jovial toasts to solemn
ceremonies.

The Bible makes little reference to blessings during
weddings. There is one biblical reference to blessing at a wedding supper. John said that "those who attend the wedding
supper of the Lamb will be blessed" (Revelation 19:9).

However, the Torah (first five books of the Bible) forbids a newly married man to leave for war during the first year of marriage, so he can "bring happiness to the wife he has married" (Deuteronomy 24:5). Hebrew traditions hold that blessing a wife is part of her happiness.

Israel's elders blessed Boaz just prior to his marriage to Ruth:

> May the LORD make the woman who is coming into your home like Rachel and Leah, who together built up the house of Israel. May you have standing in Ephrathah and be famous in Bethlehem. Through the offspring the LORD gives you by this young woman, may your family be like that of Perez, whom Tamar bore to Judah.
>
> — RUTH 4:11-12

Wedding festivities are excellent times when blessings are needed, both for the couple as well as parents left in the "empty nest."

——— #7 UNITY ———

Blessing makes

two people one.

8. Spiritual Transformations

The Bible records numerous spiritual encounters or holy ambushes when blessings were spoken by God or by angels.

Jacob is a case in point. His brother's rage drove him to a desert-resting place where God appeared to him in a dream and blessed him. When Jacob awoke, he in turn blessed God and the spot he named Bethel, "House of God" (Genesis 28:10-22). Twenty years later, returning home, Jacob wrestled all night with a "man." At daybreak, the man said, "Let me go." Jacob replied, "I will not let you go unless you bless me." This requested blessing changed his name from Jacob (Supplanter) to Israel (Striver with God). As before, Jacob blessed the place of spiritual encounter by calling it Peniel, "Face of God" (Genesis 32:22-32). In both instances, Jacob spoke blessings to God and over places he regarded as holy.

The Damascus road experience not only changed Saul into Paul, but a persecutor into a blesser. Paul's later Epistles are characterized by blessing God and people.

——— #8 PURPOSE ———

Blessing deepens

newfound zeal.

9. Significant Accomplishments

Before departing on an extended trip, a man entrusted his money with three servants. To one he gave $5,000 to invest during his absence. When the man returned he learned that the wise investor had doubled his money. This accomplishment resulted in a spoken blessing: "Well done, good and faithful servant! You have been faithful with a few things; I will put you in charge of many things. Come and share your master's happiness!" (Matthew 25:21).

I gave a public blessing to my brother at a military pinning ceremony. Here is part of that blessing:

"Terrell, I bless you as Brigadier General. You command your troops with wisdom, compassion, and genuine concern. They hold you in high esteem. It is not by accident that so many were present at your Changing of the Guard Ceremony a few weeks ago.

I have spoken with some of those under your command. They admire and follow you, not out of duty but out of respect.

You and I have fought many battles together when I was your bigger brother. Now, I will be proud to follow you in any battle as my leader.

"I bless you as my brother.

"You have always been there for me. I have benefited from your wisdom, counsel, and generosity. You even gave me part of your inheritance. There is a bond that exists between us that has nothing to do with accomplishments, status, or money. It is a covenant bond that says 'What is mine is yours, and what is yours is mine.' I bless you as a generous and unselfish brother."

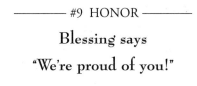

──────── #9 HONOR ────────

Blessing says

"We're proud of you!"

10. Illness

Sickness, whether long or brief, interrupts daily routines for both patient and family. A prolonged sickness can create guilt, grief, and anger in the patient. Frequent blessings spoken by family and friends during sickness can bring reassurance and set a positive environment that will aid the healing process.

The Bible gives two accounts of a king in Israel who had a terminal illness. Upon learning of his imminent death, Hezekiah called out to God and wept bitterly. Isaiah then blessed the sick king with words from God; in three days Hezekiah was completely well.

> I have heard your prayer and seen your tears; I will add fifteen years to your life. And I will deliver you and this city from the hand of the king of Assyria. I will defend this city.
>
> — ISAIAH 38:5-6

Harvey blessed his wife during a two-week illness:

"Martha, I know you must feel badly about being in bed for several days. But I want you to know that I love you for who you are, not what you do. I understand that you are doing all you can to get well. I bless you as the woman of my life. I love you deeply and bless you with the presence of God to bring complete healing to you."

——— #10 WHOLENESS ———

Blessing eases anger, guilt and grief.

11. Retirement

Different people in different times have viewed retirement

in different ways. Work was contemptible for the ancient Greek and Roman upper classes, in sharp contrast to the Judeo-Christian understanding of work as a command from God. "Six days you shall labor and do all your work" (Exodus 20:9).

Historically, most people died in their 30s or 40s, excluding the possibility of retirement. However, since current life expectancy in industrial nations has more than doubled, people must plan the years after leaving vocational jobs.

Retirement does bring radical change for most people—from exhilarating freedom to debilitating boredom. This sudden routine adjustment can be minimized as family and friends bless the retiree with assuring and affirming words. At no time are blessings needed more than during the first year of retirement, especially for people whose identity has been wrapped up in their job.

——— #11 WORTH ———

Blessing reaffirms
personal value.

12. Death

Jacob's lifestyle of blessing reached a climax shortly before his death when he blessed his twelve sons the final time. These weren't insignificant rambles of an old man, but once-in-a-lifetime words that told what would "happen to you in the days to come" (Genesis 49:1). History verifies the accuracy of his prophetic blessings.

Discussing death and dying are taboos in our culture. We're uncomfortable talking about death, especially our own. This denial is portrayed when a man said to his wife,

"When one of us dies, I'm moving to Paris."

When someone dies, we often hear: "I remember the last thing they said." How significant if *our* last words are those of blessings. Like Jacob, whose blessings helped shape the life of each son, our blessings have a powerful impact on those around us, not only when we die, but also each day we live.

An old Rabbi said to his student, "Bless people the day before you die."

"But Rabbi," said a student. "I don't know the day I will die."

"Then bless people today!"

──────── #12 HERITAGE ────────

Blessing imprints

a lasting impression.

FIVE

THE MIRACLE BEGINS

PART OF THE MIRACLE of blessing is the human emotions stirred as blessings are spoken. Recent discoveries about the human brain have proven how our emotions strongly influence our behavior and capacity to learn. Stirred emotions supply the energy and drive (motivation) to accomplish plans and goals.

The connection between this ground-breaking research and the power of blessing is obvious. Blessing others and the need to be blessed are basic to who we are as emotional beings.

2 MINUTE EXERCISES

Reading this book changes nothing; you must begin practicing what you are learning. The exercises on the following pages will help open a whole new world of wholeness—both for you and those you bless.

For You

It isn't easy forgiving someone who has wronged you. But this process is quite necessary if you want to be free from encroaching resentment and destructive bitterness. Before we bless others, we must first ask ourselves if there is anyone whom we haven't fully forgiven.

Find a quite place to sit down. Close your eyes. You may want to focus on the Lord for a few minutes in order to help settle your thoughts and to begin moving your mind toward a clear, calm and receptive state. Then ask yourself if there is anyone you need to forgive. If someone enters your thoughts, begin there. Once you decide to forgive, blessing that person moves forgiveness along much more rapidly.

> Before we bless others, we must first ask if there is anyone whom we haven't fully forgiven.

These blessings can be given in person or from a distance. Either way, blessing gradually changes situations and people because of the biblical principle of forgiving—if you forgive others, God will forgive and cancel His judgment against you.

For Married Couples and Parents

Spend a few moments reflecting on your spouse and/or your children, what they mean to you. Also think about your dreams for their future. It may be helpful to jot down three or four sentences on paper that convey the blessings you have for them, thoughts easily memorized to maximize the effect of your words. Some people use an appropriate Bible verse. Find an opportunity to bless your spouse "even if it frightens her (or him) at first." Remember it is most effective if you take their hands, make eye contact, and affirm him or her with blessings.

Blessing your children may be awkward and a little uncomfortable, but it will have a great impact, especially if repeated often.

For Single Adults

Ask several friends at work to read this book. Then, during a lunch break, let everyone practice blessing each other in a manner similar to the one mentioned above. This will deepen friendships rather remarkably. Don't be surprised if someone says, "I didn't know you felt that way about me."

For Youth

Young people catch the miracle of blessing quickly. Again, pass this book around and have everyone read it. Then, practice blessing one another, using some of the same principles above. Not only will this strengthen friendships, but it can mend broken relationships.

The first time Charlotte and Angie were exposed to blessing was in a seminar we conducted in a home where they were foster children. These two teenage

> Not only will blessing strengthen friendships, but it can mend broken relationships.

girls did not get along well together. Each resisted the other and made the family environment tense and difficult for other family members.

During the afternoon session, the blessing was taught, then demonstrated for friends and family. As several people shared blessings of warmth, love, and affection, Angie suddenly left the room. Blessings continued as the Holy Spirit intensified His presence among us.

Charlotte soon slipped out and returned with Angie. She asked Angie to sit in a chair in the middle of the room. Then Charlotte sat down on the floor at Angie's feet.

"I want to ask your forgiveness for being hard to live with," Charlotte said. "I have really made it difficult for you in this home. I want to love you, but I don't know how to get along with you. I want to. Please forgive me. I see you as a beautiful person who belongs here. You have such a wonderful future. Let's give our friendship another try."

During her emotional blessing, Charlotte's tears were falling on Angie's bare feet. Picture the impact the moment Charlotte took her long blonde hair and wiped Angie's feet!

Angie arose from her chair, embraced Charlotte, confessed her own sins, and returned a blessing.

DO WHAT GOD DOES

If you've chosen to walk with God, He has *already* given you His Holy Spirit to be like Him, His mind to think like Him, and His divine nature to act like Him. However, receiving these gifts isn't enough. You must practice doing what God does. The Bible is the record book of His activities—how He thinks and acts—and sets the standard for all human thinking, speaking, and living.

It is God's nature to bless you. Therefore, as you practice blessing, His nature is developed in you. Peter reminds us that "this is what you are called to do."

There's more good news.

As you bless, you begin inheriting blessings yourself which become your greatest wealth (Proverbs 10:22, *The Living Bible*).

Bless and be blessed! It is the same principle Jesus established regarding material things.

> Give, and it will be given to you. A good measure, pressed down, shaken together and running over, will be poured into your lap. For with the measure you use, it will be measured to you.
>
> — LUKE 6:38

There is a rich storehouse of blessings awaiting you. Begin today to possess your inheritance as you walk with Him and impact people around you, often in a matter of minutes.

About the Author

M. Lynn Reddick, Ph.D., is a nationally known motivation speaker and church leadership trainer. He and his wife, Linda, travel extensively throughout North America and many foreign countries, conducting seminars on open meeting principles, small group dynamics, and life-changing blessings.

He earned a Bachelor of Arts in psychology and Christianity, a Master of Divinity, Master of Theology, Doctor of Ministry (D.Min.) and graduated *magna cum laude* with a Doctor of Philosophy (Ph.D.). In the summer of 1967, he worked on an archaeological excavation at Tel Arad, Israel, with Yohanan Aharoni where the only known temple outside of Jerusalem was discovered.

He was among innovative church leaders who developed cell groups and open meeting principles in the early 1960's. His thirty-eight year pastoral experience was preparation for today's wider ministry as president of Open Church Ministries, a network of over 100 churches. Dr. Reddick is also president of Covenant Bible Institute in Portal, Georgia.

He and his wife, Linda, have two married children and three grandchildren.